Reinventing
Your Self

Reinventing Your Self

28 Strategies for Coping With Change

Mark Towers

SkillPath Publications
Mission, Kansas

Editor: Kelly Scanlon

Cover and Book Design: Rod Hankins

Library of Congress Catalog Card Number: 95-69803

ISBN: 1-878542-90-7

10   9   8   7   6   5   4   98   99

Printed in the United States of America

Contents

Introduction

We are living in an era of "permanent white water." Our lives are fast-moving—and there's no sign of the pace letting up. In fact, the pace we maintain continues to accelerate. Change has become the norm. Consider these facts:

- Information currently doubles nearly every 900 days.

- Twenty percent of all families in America move each year.

- There are so few farmers that the U.S. Census Bureau no longer considers them a separate category.

- The fastest growing segment of the American work force is people who work from their homes.

This kind of relentless change can easily engulf us—if we aren't prepared. We need only to look at current health statistics to see the downside of trying to keep pace:

- 25 million Americans have high blood pressure.

- One million people die from heart attacks each year.

- Eight million people have stomach ulcers.

- Twelve million Americans are reported to be alcoholics.

- More than 230 million prescriptions are filled each year for tranquilizers.

But the bottom line is this: The world isn't going to slow down. Our task is to find usable strategies for reinventing our "selves" and equipping our "selves" to deal with this ongoing change. Indeed, reinventing government, business, and ourselves is a necessity if we are to survive and thrive.

This is a book about changing your "self," about keeping your "self" informed, fresh, and creative in order to cope with change. It is a book about being proactive, about meeting change head-on. It is about breaking old paradigms and shifting gears in order to remain productive, employable, and happy in a demanding world. It is a book about your future success.

This book provides twenty-eight practical and usable strategies for reinventing your "self" during these challenging times of change. The beauty of these strategies is that none of them requires you to make grand changes in your lifestyle. Rather they are more subtle, often overlooked, suggestions for nudging yourself in a new direction, for looking at life from a new perspective. In fact, many of them are simply commonsense guides to living happier, less stressful lives. Digest these strategies. Be creative with them. *Adapt* them—don't adopt them. Make them work positively for you—both at work and at home.

Excellent firms don't believe in excellence—only in constant improvement and constant change.

—Tom Peters

Ask challenging questions.

Remember that life isn't about answers. It's about questions. Indeed, it's about asking clear and candid questions that challenge your situation and assumptions. In particular, get into the habit of asking these three questions:

1. "What's going well?"

2. "What could be going better?"

3. "What should I/we consider doing to make things go even better?"

At work, ask these questions of your boss and co-workers. At home, use them with your spouse, children, and friends.

Encourage open and honest feedback—and be prepared to flex your personal style. You'll encourage honest responses if you openly show that you're willing to change. Remember, your life is defined by your actions—not by your words. Reinventing yourself means acting yourself into new ways of thinking and, therefore, being—not thinking yourself into new ways of acting.

The value of this strategy

Many people stagnate at work and at home—often without realizing it. In today's world, you can't afford to be one of those people. Reinventing yourself means consciously choosing to change yourself by constantly asking questions that challenge your thinking and your routine ways of doing things.

Life is a daring adventure

or it is really nothing

at all.

—Helen Keller

Get out of your comfort zone.

Choose a certain time once each week to plan an out-of-comfort-zone experience. Survey the week ahead of you. Pick a time, place, and event—and go for it! Schedule a hot air balloon ride. Go horseback riding. Attend a worship service of a church that you know nothing about. If you don't want to go it alone, take a friend with you. Enjoy the event together.

Let's face it. You can't expand your comfort zone if you're not having experiences outside of it. Indeed, effectively reinventing yourself means being able to step outside your current boundaries to survey some of the other things the world has to offer.

The value of this strategy

If this strategy sounds scary, just remember that you control your out-of-comfort zone experiences. You're changing, but on your own controlled terms. You're giving yourself an opportunity to get used to the "idea" of change by choosing the change.

Happiness is good health and a bad memory.

—Ingrid Bergman

Resolve to exercise.

If you're already exercising, evaluate your routine and try some different forms of exercise. If you don't follow a program, rearrange your schedule so you can make exercise a priority two or three times a week. Get up half an hour early to take a brisk walk. Take the stairs whenever possible, or park across the parking lot so you have to hike to the store.

While you're exercising and pumping more oxygen to your brain, think about your life, your priorities, and your aspirations.

With each leg lift, push up, or backstroke, push worry and doubt out and away. Think to yourself: "There's no problem or situation that I can't address."

Ease yourself into your exercise program—particularly if you haven't been exercising at all. Remember this little jingle: "Inch by inch, life is a cinch. Yard by yard, life is hard." View your commitment to exercise as a long-term paradigm shift—not as a "health" kick.

The value of this strategy

The psychology here is quite simple. Of course, exercise for the physical benefits. But exercise for the mental payoffs as well! Assuredly, many creative people report that their best ideas come while exercising.

You can't be as receptive to or accepting of change and demands if you're tired, stressed, or sick. Following a regular exercise program will help you to stay healthy, fit, alert, and ready to meet change head-on.

We do not
remember days,
we remember
moments.

—**Cesare Pavese**

Stage a key event for your co-workers or the members of an organization you belong to.

Have a tea party; serve no coffee, soft drinks, or alcohol. Provide light snacks. Choose an unusual setting for the party such as an art gallery or a community service center. If a tea party seems too formal, try a camping outing or a picnic in a nearby park.

Get the ball rolling by asking prospective attendees what type of outing they'd prefer. Ingest their input, but remember to put your own creative spin on the event too. Door prizes, skits, stunts, and group activities always create meaningful memories.

Be a gracious host and use the party to help people relax and work in a refreshing, comfortable setting. The purpose is to invite them into an arena of thoughtfulness away from the typical fast-paced, let's-get-this-done-now frenzied atmosphere.

Plan your agenda well. Give away at least one door prize during the event. Emphasize the dialogue and social aspects of the meeting as much as the tasks to be completed. Above all, focus the attention on the people who attend—not on yourself. Be sure to thank everyone for coming.

The value of this strategy

Many people are promoted (or demoted) for their ability to handle key events. Proactively staging a key event indicates that you're committed to making a difference in other people's lives.

W

isdom is the reward you get for a lifetime of listening when you'd have preferred to talk.

—Doug Larsen

Listen.

Learn to be an active listener. Yes, everyone enjoys being center stage. When you listen intently to others, you give them the opportunity to shine in the spotlight. You send a message that you care, that what the other person has to say is important. Furthermore, you'll feel better about yourself for taking the time and making the effort to focus on other folks. Remember, it's impossible to learn anything new while you are talking. When you find yourself talking too much, remember this: The word *listen* and the word *silent* contain the same six letters.

When others are speaking, make a conscious effort to really *hear* what they're saying. Many times when we think we're listening, we're really caught up in our own thoughts. When this happens, it's easy to tune others out. Resolve to pay closer attention when others are speaking. Here are some tips for tuning in:

- Concentrate on the speaker's entire means of expression. Watch for facial and body cues.

- Take notes to keep focused on the speaker's message.

- Repeat what the speaker says, using your own words.

- Only after the speaker stops should you speak, and then only after you've taken a moment to consider your response.

The value of this strategy

Listening takes your mind off your own problems and helps you focus on something else. Often, hearing about the troubles of others makes your own challenges seem trivial in comparison. Plus, you'll be amazed at the wealth of ideas you will pick up when you give others a chance to express themselves.

Y*ou are today where your thoughts have brought you; you will be tomorrow where your thoughts take you.*

—James Allen

Stay up all night.

Sustain yourself with a little bit of food (soup or something light) and drink (no alcohol).

Don't read, watch television, listen to the radio, or talk to anyone else. Simply go inside yourself. Find silence, write down your best thoughts, and then enjoy the beautiful sunrise.

Since you'll be losing a night's sleep, carefully plan this experience. Survey the next two months and choose the appropriate day and night for this experience.

The value of this strategy

This type of introspection allows you to see yourself from an angle that you never really consider—one that's free of busy schedules and deadlines, one that's not tied to a particular role (spouse, parent, boss, PTA president). You're alone with you. Don't fret about losing sleep— you can catch up later.

The trouble with life in the fast lane is that you get to the other end in an awful hurry.

—John Jensen

Make "breathing space" for yourself to slow down and rethink your priorities.

Don't watch the evening news. Watch the sunset instead. Bask in the *slowness* of this event!

The evening news epitomizes the fast lane—the world of daily bumps and grinds. Images swirl past us as footage, and we remember messages from leaders as sound bytes. Often, our own lives follow a similar pattern as we rush from event to event, focusing simply on the highlights and not taking the time to relish in the whole experience.

The value of this strategy

Take a clue from the things that occur naturally around you. Sometimes to find beauty and meaning we must be patient; we must take the time to observe. Think how deprived we'd be if the sunset faded as quickly as a 30-second sound byte. Yet too often that's all the time we give ourselves to reflect on our daily events.

The genius of life

is being able to

take childhood

into old age.

—George Burns

Find a place in your life for laughter, humor, and play.

Laughter, play, and humor are all close cousins of creativity. It's important to stay loose during times of change so we can deal with our challenges creatively.

Do you know that four-year-old children laugh 385 times a day? Take a child to an amusement park. Mimic the antics of the child. Literally recreate your childhood and enjoy yourself as much as the child does.

Make a habit of collecting things that make you laugh. Keep them in a humor file. Flip through the file whenever you get the urge.

The value of this strategy

During times of change, you must often search for creative answers. Remember that laughter, play, and humor are helpful tools. When you make a mistake or experience a setback, learn to chuckle at your situation. The ability to see life with a comic vision ensures psychological health.

*S*ometimes the most urgent and vital thing you can possibly do is take a complete rest.

—Ashleigh Brilliant

Stay in bed all day.

Pamper yourself. Don't cook. Don't clean. Eat in bed. Watch a lot of television; use your remote control and "channel surf" to your heart's content! Nap. Smile. Make phone calls to people you don't normally call. Read. Above all, don't feel guilty!

Do things that allow you to experience complete rest and, in turn, joy. Note any innovative ideas that come to you.

Don't wait until you are absolutely exhausted to find time for rest. Make a place for it in your schedule now.

The value of this strategy

Weightlifters' muscles grow when they are at rest—not while they are "pumping iron" in the gym. Use the same psychology here—make the time to rest, grow, and reinvent. View this relaxation as a time to mentally grow.

Remember, no one can make you feel inferior without your consent.

—Eleanor Roosevelt

Make a list of your top six personal strengths.

Draw a line at the bottom of the list, and below the line write down three items you regard as personal weaknesses. Keep the list posted on your bathroom mirror. As you read your strengths and weaknesses as you ready yourself for work each day, brainstorm ways to hold on to the strengths (maximize your gains and potential) and simultaneously turn the weaknesses into strengths.

Write down your ideas and develop an action plan for improving yourself. Work on a different area each day. Celebrate the fact that you are discontented with certain aspects of yourself! It's definitely a positive sign that you're openly and honestly working on yourself. But remember to work from and stay focused on your strengths as you develop your plan. When you've completed your plan, tape it to the mirror as well.

Continue this process for several weeks, building on the progress you made the previous week. Don't concentrate on all new areas each week. Plan to reinforce some of the areas you identified previously. Progress takes practice.

The value of this strategy

One of the great basketball players of all time, Larry Bird of the Boston Celtics, was once asked how he became a great player. He replied, "I simply went to the gym and turned my weaknesses into strengths through practice." His words are the key to why he became such a great athlete. He wasn't blessed with "raw talent." He simply had the desire to better himself.

Those people who

ignore history are

bound to repeat it.

—Anonymous

Volunteer at a nursing home.

Talk to the residents about their pasts and what they would do differently if they had their lives to live all over again.

As you interact with the residents, you'll be surprised at how many stories they have to tell. This is a golden opportunity to practice your active listening skills.

Listen closely and collect the real wisdom these folks have lived—not just theorized. Many of them have had to adjust to their own share of change and cope with major life disruptions. Find out how they coped with the loss of loved ones or how they found the courage to face financial trauma. Avoid getting drawn into telling your personal story. Find out what they would do differently if they had to do it all over again.

The value of this strategy

The voice of experience is always a worthwhile and eye-opening teacher. By seeking first-hand knowledge from these people, you will grow. Plus, you'll have effectively served some people who are often in need of simple conversation.

W

hen the student
is ready, the teacher
will appear.

—Confucius

Be a mentor.

Consider spending some time helping a new co-worker learn the ropes. Or invite students from the local college to spend a day on the job with you. Other possibilities are becoming a Big Brother or Big Sister or volunteering to lead a youth group.

The value of this strategy

Share your knowledge with these people. To lead people literally means to educate them so they can work on their own. During times of rampant change and reinvention, society needs people (like you!) who can educate people, not control them.

Y

ou have not done enough,
you have never done
enough, so long as it is
possible that you have
something to contribute.

—Dag Hammarskjöld

Volunteer to take on a project that nobody else wants to do.

Often these distasteful tasks are critical, must-get-done projects within organizations. Being proactive and pitching in as a team player is the key sign of a highly effective and psychologically healthy individual. When you feel frustrated or exasperated as you are taking on new challenges, simply remember that you cannot learn or grow from experiences you're not having. Pitching in and being in charge of a project that no one else wants can help you learn more about other aspects of your organization.

The value of this strategy

Offering to learn how to do a new task, to "cross-train," shows that you are willing to reinvent yourself to keep pace with your organization and its needs.

Personally, I'm always ready to learn, although I do not always like being taught.

—**Winston Churchill**

Find a mentor.

Ask someone you admire and respect to be your mentor. Use this person as a sounding board for your ideas. Ask your mentor to share his or her "secrets of success." Value and respect your mentor's time. Carefully plan your agenda for meetings with this person. Furthermore, show your appreciation to your mentor on a regular basis. Send thank you notes and small gifts when appropriate. Better yet, reciprocate when you can by introducing your mentor to your own contacts who could be valuable resources, clip news items that may be of interest, or pass along information related to your mentor's hobbies and interests. See yourself as a sponge—"soak up" all you can from this valuable asset.

The value of this strategy

When successful people talk or write about how they became successful, they nearly always mention the importance of having a mentor. A mentor can "show you the ropes" quickly, help you make important connections and give you a jump by sharing the knowledge they've acquired through years of experience.

Live your life

as a play.

—Plato

STRATEGY

Consciously break your habits and routines.

We are creatures of habit. Breaking habits can help you think more creatively; trying new things can give you fresh insights. Here are some suggestions for getting started:

- Travel to work using a different route or method of transportation.

- Skip your morning coffee or tea.

- For one day, don't read the same magazine and newspapers you're accustomed to reading. Pick up something totally new and different—something you would never consider reading or scanning.

- Listen to a different type of radio or television station—something you normally don't care to hear or watch.

- Get up earlier than usual in the morning.

- Fast for a day. Don't eat any meals. Simply drink a nourishing juice.

This strategy is a bit like Strategy #2, moving out of your comfort zone, but it focuses more on your daily routine.

Start slowly. Choose a habit or routine that appears to be relatively easy to break or reverse. Experience success first. Then continue to experiment with changing more "entrenched" behaviors.

The value of this strategy

Breaking old habits and trying new things or approaches gives you a fresh perspective on the world. Breaking habits also helps you stay flexible, which is a vital tool for coping with change. Some people are constantly consumed with making their lives neat and tidy and encounter frustration at every turn. That's because something is always happening that upsets their "plans": a child gets sick, a co-worker quits—the list goes on. If you're already used to breaking your routine, you'll be able to adapt much more quickly to these unforeseen changes.

Every organization has to prepare to abandon everything it does.

—Peter Drucker

Find ways to wrap more value around the product or service you're responsible for producing.

Hanging on to antiquated, outdated systems and processes can be costly. Put to rest forever the old adage "But, we've always done it this way." Question, question, question how you're doing things and why. As you question, think about becoming more results-oriented and less systems-oriented. Get visual here. Sketch in great detail on a large piece of paper the process you use to deliver your goods and services. Get people's input about how to streamline and simplify things for the people you serve. Follow this motto: "If it doesn't add value, let's get rid of it!"

The value of this strategy

Being customer-driven rather than procedures-driven puts the emphasis on service, a key to success in today's world. Finding new ways to delight customers can only make your overall worth in the marketplace skyrocket.

I may not be the man I want to be.
I may not be the man I ought to be;
I may not be the man I could be;
I may not be the man I can be;
but praise God,
I'm not the man
I once was.

—Martin Luther King

Keep a diary.

Find ten minutes each day to write in your diary. Choose a time when you won't be distracted or feel rushed. Think over your day. Study your thoughts and your idiosyncrasies. Review your past entries. How have you changed? How have you grown?

The value of this strategy

Keeping a diary forces you to think about what's going on in your life. Furthermore, a diary provides a written record. In it, you can capture thoughts that might otherwise have been fleeting. You can watch as your thoughts and opinions evolve and change. And you also can trace the events that may have shaped that change.

I *am still learning.*

—**Michelangelo**

Read from a book fifteen minutes a day.

Reading fifteen minutes a day will net you fifteen books a year. Imagine what you can learn by reading that many books every year.

Leaders are readers. In fact, the people listed in *Who's Who in America* read an average of twenty-one books a year! On a sadder note, 58 percent of Americans who graduate from high school or college never read another nonfiction book the rest of their lives!

The value of this strategy

To get ahead, you must make learning a life-long proposition. In order to "go for it," you've also got to "grow for it!" Read. Read. Read.

The deepest principle of

Human Nature is the

craving to be appreciated.

—William James

Become a better note-writer.

Very few people take the time to write notes of appreciation. Whenever possible, write PIGS notes. PIGS is an acronym for Positive, Immediate, Graphic, and Specific. Let's break this concept down further.

***P** is for Positive.* Obviously, people love to receive notes of encouragement, congratulations, and praise.

***I** is for Immediate.* Write the note and send it within 48 hours of the event or achievement you're praising.

***G** is for Graphic.* This means handwritten. Write legibly and enclose the note in an envelope.

***S** is for Specific,* the most critical portion of the note. Look for at least *two specific details* you can incorporate into your note.

Use a sign-off phrase that makes people feel great:

"You're top flight!"

"You're the greatest!"

"All the best!"

Here's an example: Let's say your administrative assistant did a great job typing a report. You could send him a PIGS note that says: "Greg, you were two days under deadline, and there were no typos!"

The value of this strategy

It's a known fact that George Bush sent notes of appreciation throughout his career. He's been quoted as saying that note-writing was a big factor in his success and ultimately in his climb to the presidency. Taking the time to write short notes is a small change in your daily routine, but it can have big payoffs. And here's an added benefit you may not have thought of: Your notes of encouragement may very well change the lives of the receivers. Your bit of praise may give them that extra shot of confidence they need to pursue their ambitions.

That which does not kill you can only make you stronger.

—Nietzsche

See an opportunity in every challenge.

Whenever something negative happens, respond to the bad news in a positive way instead of cursing or bad-mouthing it. There's an upside to every misfortune, a kernel of benefit in every setback. Try to find at least one positive aspect of every difficult situation, even if it's the learning and growth you must go through to resolve the situation.

The value of this strategy

This strategy may seem a bit extreme. However, there's nothing wrong with not wasting time and energy dwelling on events that are beyond your control. In fact, finding at least one positive thing about the situation will help you better manage it and actively work toward a solution. You will have chosen to act rather than to be acted upon.

W

orry is negative

goal-setting.

—Anonymous

Keep a daily worry list.

Write down things that worry you. Spend three minutes each day worrying—intensely worrying (it's better to do this late in the evening when you have a full day's events to dwell on). Put yourself into absolute misery! After three minutes, rip up the worry list and go on with your life and the business at hand.

The value of this strategy

Extended worrying can rob you of precious energy; futhermore, it doesn't help you deal with change. It is much more practical to quickly put the past behind you and to focus on what lies in front of you. Too much rehashing of bygone events is much like spending hours reading yesterday's newspapers. Get on with your life by running toward present-day challenges. If you run toward them, they won't be able to sneak up on you from behind.

Look around you and you'll agree that the really happy people are those who have broken the chains of procrastination. Those who find satisfaction in doing the job at hand. They're full of eagerness, zest, productivity. You can be, too.

—Norman Vincent Peale

Make a conscious choice to turn up your energy level.

Pretend you have an imaginary "reset button" on your right elbow or on something that you always carry with you, such as your ring, watch, or glasses. When you need a boost of energy, simply touch this imaginary reset button. This is your clue to straighten your posture, open your eyes wider, and project yourself more assertively. Imagine a powerful energy surge moving throughout your entire body. Now you have psychologically prepared yourself to better deal with the situation at hand! Remember that you always have the option of "resetting yourself" to tackle the challenges in your path.

The value of this strategy

In today's demanding world, you must have a healthy supply of stamina. Think of yourself as a professional athlete who must always be prepared to compete. Being able to mentally maneuver yourself into readiness is an absolute necessity. It will give you the slight edge you need to cope with the challenges you encounter each day.

Excellence is to

do a common

thing in an

uncommon way.

—Booker T. Washington

Continually seek the creative or competitive advantage.

There are five competitive advantages—more, better, faster, different, or cheaper (less expensive). Brainstorm ways you can deliver these advantages to others. Remember, we are living in intensely competitive times. The ability to do a common thing in an uncommon way is very important in today's world.

Here are some examples of how people have done some common things in uncommon ways:

- A woman enclosed a tea bag in each envelope that she sent to her prospective clients (the competitive advantage of different).

- A woman made a postcard with her picture on the front (easy to do at any print shop). When someone inquired about her consulting services, she returned the call, and then followed up with a postcard too (the competitive advantages of more and different).

- Two men running a small business decided to use Federal Express to send lengthy and important correspondence to their customers. They wanted their customers to get it the next day (the competitive advantage of faster).

The value of this strategy

Constantly seeking new ways is a form of improvement. The Japanese have a word for continual improvement: *kaizen*. It means to strive for small improvements each and every day. When you seek to improve, you're being proactive; the ball is in your court, so to speak. If you wait until circumstances force you to seek new ways, change will be intimidating.

*T*ime is a circus

always packing up

and moving away.

—Ben Hecht

Work smarter, not harder.

How often have you heard that advice? Do you know what it really means? How to put it into action? Here are five ways you can work smarter—and reinvent yourself in the process:

- *The Anticipator's Approach:* Set early, artificial deadlines. Be a bit early to all appointments. Make promptness a way of life! Adopt this motto: If you're not early, you're late.

- *The Tag-Team Approach:* Always have a good friend or co-worker you can rely on. Pledge to tackle problems together.

- *The Bunch-and-Batch Approach:* Bunch and batch similar priorities and tasks. Return all your phone calls at one time. Write all your memos at one sitting. Run all your errands during one outing.

- *The All Habits-Are-Not-Bad Approach:* Stick to your high-payoff habits. These may include exercising every morning before you go to work, making your To Do list at the end of each day, or reading two bedtime stories to your toddler.

- *High-Tech Approach:* Use technology that helps you get things done faster. Fax machines, car phones, and laptop computers continue to help people be more productive.

Log your time for ten working days. Study how you use your time and then apply these five ways of working smarter to improve your situation.

The value of this strategy

Time is our most precious commodity. It can't be stored, saved, or borrowed; it can only be filled with activities. Any improvement in your approach to managing time is always a high payoff.

K

nowledge is happiness, because to have knowledge—broad, deep knowledge—is to know true ends from false, and lofty things from low. To know the thoughts and deeds that have marked man's progress is to feel the great heart-throbs of humanity through the centuries; and if one does not feel in these pulsations a heavenward striving, one must indeed be deaf to the harmonies of life.

—Helen Keller

Master a skill.

Learn how to masterfully cook an omelet, play a guitar, or race a motorcycle. Delve deeply into an area you have a strong passion for. Study and learn all that you can. Enjoy the frustrations as well as the successes that you experience as you immerse yourself into this learning. Find others who have become masters in your chosen area and ask one of them to become your mentor.

The value of this strategy

If you make mastery your goal, you will never be satisfied with mediocrity. You'll continually strive for excellence and challenge yourself to do so. Again, *you'll* be in control of change. You'll have the upperhand because you will have *chosen* to change; you won't have been *forced* to.

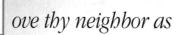

*L*ove thy neighbor as

thyself, but choose

your neighborhood.

—Louise Beal

Surround yourself with forward-thinking people.

Don't spend all your time working with people who resist change and don't want to improve themselves. Work with people on the leading edge—people like you who truly want to reinvent themselves. The people who want to catch up will do so eventually.

People do things for their own reasons—not yours. Be content with that notion.

Keep a mental or written list of the movers and shakers in your organization. Look to create opportunities to work with these folks whenever possible. These are the people who will sustain you and keep you excited about coming to work.

The value of this strategy

There is a great deal of truth in this notion: You're known by the company you keep. In times of perpetual change and transition, it is best to ally yourself with people who actively seek change rather than with those who fight it.

There are two tragedies in life. One is to lose your heart's desire. The other is to gain it.

—George Bernard Shaw

Set meaningful goals.

People often set too many goals. They think they are going to reinvent themselves instantly. It doesn't work that way. Goal-setting involves introspection and commitment to following through.

Here is the key to this strategy: Never set more than five goals in any one year. A short list of goals will allow you to stay more focused on the areas of your life that are important to you—family, friends, faith, productivity, and health, for example. If you strive toward too many goals, you may very well overextend yourself or create so much pressure that you end up taking no action.

Set one personal goal, one work-related goal, and at least one leisure-related goal each year. These three goals will keep you focused on what it is you are trying to accomplish.

Break the goals into action, description, and deadline "chunks." Commit to your calendar the steps you will have to take to achieve these goals.

Use the following outline to write your goals on paper:

Personal:

I will _____ (action) in order to

_____ (description) by

_____ (deadline).

Example: I will train (action) in order to run a ten-kilometer race in under 50 minutes (description) by October 15 of this year (deadline).

Work-related:

I will _____ (action) in order to

_____ (description) by

_____ (deadline).

Example: I will study (action) in order to pass my supervisor's test (description) by July 15 of this year (deadline).

Leisure-related:

I will _____ (action) in order to

_____ (description) by

_____ (deadline).

Example: I will plan our vacation with a travel agent (action) in order to take my family on an eight-day vacation to the Caribbean (description) during the week of August 15 of this year (deadline).

The value of this strategy

One final word about goal setting. If you don't achieve a goal, it is not the end of the world. Remember, it was simply a target that you were trying to hit. The bottom line: Missing a goal should never ruin your self-esteem. It is simply better to be guided by goals, not governed by them!

The quotations when engraved upon the memory give you good thoughts. They also make you anxious to read the authors and look for more.

—Winston Churchill

Read and memorize
meaningful quotations.

Dig deep into books of quotations and the biographies of people who changed the course of history. Collect their terrific "sound bytes" from the past and the present. Share them with others because they help us all deal with our present realities and with the future. They give us the strength and the courage to carry on and to reinvent ourselves.

The value of this strategy

Inspirational words from others is what often provides people with the impetus to leave their complacency and reinvent themselves. These "words to live by" can serve as great motivators.

The Reinvention Checklist

Place a check next to "yes" or "no" for each question. If you are able to check "yes" to all ten items, you are ready, willing, and able to begin reinventing yourself.

Yes ____ No ____   1. I understand that reinventing myself is critical to my survival. I cannot simply be content with the status quo.

Yes ____ No ____   2. I understand that reinventing myself will take commitment and struggle. It is not easy work.

Yes ____ No ____   3. I understand that I may need to seek the help and support of others as I reinvent myself.

Yes ____ No ____   4. I understand that I will need to motivate myself and maintain a positive attitude as I reinvent myself.

Yes ____ No ____   5. I understand that I will have to make learning a life-long commitment in order to reinvent myself.

Yes ____ No ____   6. I understand that others may scoff at me or question some of my behaviors as I reinvent myself, but I will have the courage to carry on.

Yes ____ No ____   7. I understand that I will have to expand my comfort zone and embrace a wider array of experiences in order to effectively reinvent myself.

Yes ____ No ____   8. I understand that I am perfectly fine just the way I am. However, I am contentedly discontent. I want to maximize my potential.

Yes ____ No ____   9. I understand that it's perfectly fine for me to get excited about reinventing myself and, in turn, transfer my excitement to others.

Yes ____ No ____   10. I understand that my life will be defined by my actions—not by my words.

Bibliography

Block, Peter. *The Empowered Manager: Positive Political Skills at Work*. San Francisco: Jossey-Bass, 1987.

Byhan, William, and Jeff Cos. *Zapp! The Lightning of Empowerment: How to Improve Productivity, Quality and Employee Satisfaction*. New York: Ballantine Books, 1988.

Covey, Stephen R. *The Seven Habits of Highly Effective People: Restoring the Character Ethic.* New York: Simon and Schuster, 1990.

Edelsom, Martin. *I-Power: The Secrets of Great Business in Bad Times*. Fort Lee, NJ: Barricade Books, 1992.

Garfield, Charles. *Second to None: How Our Smartest Companies Put People First*. Homewood, IL: Business One Irwin, 1992.

Kragen, Ken. *Life Is a Contact Sport: Ten Great Strategies That Work*. New York: W. Morrow, 1994.

Manz, Charles, and Henry Sims. *Business Without Bosses: How Self-Managing Teams Are Building High Performance Companies*. New York: Wiley, 1993.

Peters, Tom. *Crazy Times Call for Crazy Organizations*. New York: Vintage Books, 1994.

Senge, Peter. *The Fifth Discipline: The Art and Practice of the Learning Organization*. New York: Doubleday/Currency, 1990.

Silver, Susan. *Organized to Be the Best! New Timesaving Ways to Simplify and Improve How You Work.* Los Angeles: Adams-Hall, 1991.

Stack, Jack. *The Great Game of Business.* New York: Doubleday/Currency, 1992.

Towers, Mark. *The ABC's of Empowered Teams: Building Blocks for Success.* Mission, KS: SkillPath Publications, 1994.

Towers, Mark. *Dynamic Delegation: A Manager's Guide for Active Empowerment.* Mission, KS: SkillPath Publications, 1993.

Available From SkillPath Publications

Self-Study Sourcebooks

Climbing the Corporate Ladder: What You Need to Know and Do to Be a Promotable Person *by Barbara Pachter and Marjorie Brody*

Coping With Supervisory Nightmares: 12 Common Nightmares of Leadership and What You Can Do About Them *by Michael and Deborah Singer Dobson*

Defeating Procrastination: 52 Fail-Safe Tips for Keeping Time on Your Side *by Marlene Caroselli, Ed.D.*

Discovering Your Purpose *by Ivy Haley*

Going for the Gold: Winning the Gold Medal for Financial Independence *by Lesley D. Bissett, CFP*

Having Something to Say When You Have to Say Something: The Art of Organizing Your Presentation *by Randy Horn*

Info-Flood: How to Swim in a Sea of Information Without Going Under *by Marlene Caroselli, Ed.D.*

The Innovative Secretary *by Marlene Caroselli, Ed.D.*

Letters & Memos: Just Like That! *by Dave Davies*

Mastering the Art of Communication: Your Keys to Developing a More Effective Personal Style *by Michelle Fairfield Poley*

Organized for Success! 95 Tips for Taking Control of Your Time, Your Space, and Your Life *by Nanci McGraw*

A Passion to Lead! How to Develop Your Natural Leadership Ability *by Michael Plumstead*

P.E.R.S.U.A.D.E.: Communication Strategies That Move People to Action *by Marlene Caroselli, Ed.D.*

Productivity Power: 250 Great Ideas for Being More Productive *by Jim Temme*

Promoting Yourself: 50 Ways to Increase Your Prestige, Power, and Paycheck *by Marlene Caroselli, Ed.D.*

Proof Positive: How to Find Errors Before They Embarrass You *by Karen L. Anderson*

Risk-Taking: 50 Ways to Turn Risks Into Rewards *by Marlene Caroselli, Ed.D. and David Harris*

Speak Up and Stand Out: How to Make Effective Presentations *by Nanci McGraw*

Stress Control: How You Can Find Relief From Life's Daily Stress *by Steve Bell*

The Technical Writer's Guide *by Robert McGraw*

Total Quality Customer Service: How to Make It Your Way of Life *by Jim Temme*

Write It Right! A Guide for Clear and Correct Writing *by Richard Andersen and Helene Hinis*

Your Total Communication Image *by Janet Signe Olson, Ph.D.*

Handbooks

The ABC's of Empowered Teams: Building Blocks for Success *by Mark Towers*

Assert Yourself! Developing Power-Packed Communication Skills to Make Your Points Clearly, Confidently, and Persuasively *by Lisa Contini*

For more information, call 1-800-873-7545.

NOTES

NOTES